SCRIPTURE PASSAGES THAT *changed* MY LIFE

PERSONAL STORIES FROM THE WRITERS OF

*Living***Faith**

TWENTY-THIRD PUBLICATIONS
twentythirdpublications.com

TWENTY-THIRD PUBLICATIONS
One Montauk Avenue, Suite 200
New London, CT 06320
(860) 437-3012 or (800) 321-0411
www.twentythirdpublications.com

Cover photo: © Shutterstock / robert_s

ISBN: 978-1-62785-356-9
Library of Congress Control Number: 2017960972
Printed in the U.S.A.

 A division of Bayard, Inc.

Contents

Introduction

The title of this book, *Scripture Passages That Changed My Life*, could be misleading. The reason being, as strictly a matter of fact, the verses themselves didn't change the lives of the authors. Their lives were changed because they chose to receive the words that were put before them. They chose to act upon them because the word of God penetrated their heart and soul.

This is not merely a matter of semantics. God is amazingly good to us in granting us the gift of free will. Our free will determines our thinking and our behavior. God is kind and patient, knowing full well that we, unfortunately, often choose to stray.

Maybe a more accurate description of the stories that follow would be, "How I Chose to *Allow* These Scripture Passages to Change My Life"! And by choosing what we read, we place our trust in an author, allowing them to lead us places.

The ten *Living Faith* authors featured in this book have related their very personal and moving experiences with the word of God on the pages that follow. We are confident that by choosing to read these essays, your trust in the authors will be rewarded. We further hope that these writings will bring you closer to the author of all life, our loving God. May you be enriched and strengthened by the inspiring words that you will find on the following pages. They just might change your life—if you let them.

TERENCE HEGARTY, *editor*

Micah 6:8

You have been told,
O mortal, what is good,
and what the Lord
requires of you:
Only to do justice
and to love goodness,
and to walk humbly
with your God.

ONLY THIS

by **Chris Koellhoffer, IHM**

One of my earliest memories of an encounter with God came when I was five years old. Can one experience a mystic moment at that tender age? I believe so, for children have a way of getting right to the heart of things. Children have a purity of vision unobstructed by cynicism or by the jaded sense of having already experienced all there is to see.

Our family lived in the suburbs of New Jersey, surrounded by our cherished friends in the plant and animal worlds, at a time when there was minimal artificial lighting. Sometimes, in the early hours past midnight, our dad would shake us awake, wrap us in blankets and carry us out to the deck on the second floor. From that vantage point, we could glance down at the darkened homes in the valley below. Even better, we could gaze upward at a night sky brilliant with stars. While still rubbing sleep from our eyes, we would rest there, silenced by the immensity looking back at us. We simply basked in wonder and awe in the hush of the evening. We felt the inadequacy of words but intuited that we were in the presence of the Holy.

Dad told us that our names were written in the heavens. I was just learning to read, but with serious squinting, I was so sure I could find the stars that spelled "Chris." A thousand astronomers could not have convinced me otherwise. What we experienced on those still nights was a palpable sense of a universe that was beyond our understanding and, at the same time, alive with the presence of a Creator who felt incredibly close, familiar, and intimate. In those formative years, the path to the Holy seemed amazingly simple and straightforward. Open your ears, open your eyes, open your heart. Listen and pay attention to Holy Mystery at work in the world.

And then, I became a sophisticated teenager, at least in my own estimation. In high school and as a young adult, I was caught up in a self-imposed notion of perfection, as if everything depended on me. As if perfection were what God was expecting of me. No, *demanding* of me. Living with that naïve, youthful perspective, I was doomed to failure, given the flaws and limits of the human condition. Only very slowly did I grow into an understanding of spirituality and of what it was that God truly desired of me and for me. I consider it grace that, at some point when I was struggling to live out of my misinformed concept of God's expectations, I bumped up against the words of the prophet Micah. These words seemed to leap off the page and straight into my heart:

> You have been told, O mortal, what is good,
> and what the Lord requires of you:

Only to do justice and to love goodness,
and to walk humbly with your God.
MICAH 6:8

Those words both intrigued and disturbed me. They became a catalyst of sorts, propelling me forward into a more tender, less judgmental direction. Micah's wisdom reoriented me and, like the stars, nudged me to navigate the universe with fresh thinking. My carefully crafted path to God, a path where I once thought every step must be calculated and measured, was crumbling under my feet. Was it possible that the spiritual life was a lot simpler—although not easier—than I had ever imagined? Micah's words suggested that my emphasis had been misplaced, for the path to the Holy, clearly, wasn't about only me and my solitary efforts. It wasn't about how perfectly I could offer sacrifice or recite a lengthy list of prayers. It was about right relationship with God, with others, with myself. It was much more about discovering who God was and who I was in relationship to the Divine and all of creation. It was about how the Holy longed to live and act in me and through me and how I was cooperating with grace.

I sat with the question, *Just what does God desire of me?* and broke open the prophet's reply: "Only this: to act justly, to love tenderly, and to walk humbly with our

God." *Only* this! It sounds so simple, so straightfor-ward, as clear as sitting in contemplation in the middle of the night and drinking in the stars. Simple, yes; easy, no! The work of a lifetime.

Micah underscores that a loving God has shared with us, in words plain and clear, how to live, how to be, how to move forward as a loving person commit-ted to help bring about the fullness of life God dreams for each of us. As the prophet noted in the passage preceding Micah 6:8, our lives are not about rooting around for the perfect gift or looking to appease a dis-tant deity as we try to ward off divine judgment. It's about the invitation to reflect on right relationship between ourselves and others, between the Divine and our very human hearts; the invitation to be fair and just in our attitudes and our actions; the invitation to cultivate tender and compassionate hearts, especially toward those who are most fragile and vulnerable. And at times that may be us.

TO DO JUSTICE

The profoundly spiritual late nights of childhood stargazing prepared me for a stretching of my world-view as time moved on. After all, the same brilliant stars that looked down, as a five-year-old in suburban New Jersey was contemplating the night sky, also shed their light extravagantly in other corners of our world. Those same stars could connect to the laborer in a sweatshop, to the farmer harvesting rice in a paddy, to the girl child trafficked, separated, and cut off from hope, to the single parent struggling, paycheck to paycheck, to put food on the table.

Micah's words remind us that every event and experience of our lives takes place in the arena of justice, where nothing—no word, no attitude, no action—is without consequence. Where and how we spend our time indicates our priorities. What we choose to buy or listen to or companion is telling of what we value most. Micah calls us to live with a deepening consciousness of our place in the Earth community and of how our words and actions have both a local and a global impact.

TO LOVE GOODNESS

To be spiritual is to be open to amazement. Hopefully, we have had many experiences—like my childhood starwatch—that astonish and stun us, that suddenly and immediately expand our borders and defy easy description or categorization. We may witness in others a largeness of heart that haunts us, that shakes us awake, that simply will not let us go. We may be overwhelmed and deeply touched by those who, day in and day out, give their lives over with extraordinary and extravagant love, contributing to the fulfillment of God's dream of abundant life for all people.

Often, an experience of beauty or a bumping into wonder is an invitation for that kind of illumination. The beautiful as a reflection of divinity calls us out of ourselves. It upends the seeming ordinariness of human experience and challenges us to live fully awake and aware of God at work in our world. In experiencing goodness and beauty, we're called to admire and resonate with the artist struggling to put paint to canvas or to bring words to life or to transform sounds into haunting melody.

TO WALK HUMBLY WITH YOUR GOD

My own heart has been broken open and tenderized by walking humbly in the company of the holy ones who reveal the face of God. I have met them in Chatham, in the South Bronx, in Scranton, in San Salvador, and in Port-au-Prince. I have met them in Lima and Mexico City and every place in our world where my feet and God's grace have taken me. These holy ones have welcomed me into cardboard shacks, into tents, classrooms, kitchens, and pews. I have been graced to be with them in their art studios and circles of prayer. They have forgiven my ignorance and immersed me in cultures not my own. They have invited me into a profound solidarity as I have learned their names and their stories, as they have appreciated mine. They have inspired me to "waste" time on what really matters. They are bearers of wisdom, extraordinary teachers who have spurred me to walk on the two feet of justice—charity and advocacy—and to pay attention to the signs of the times, God's unfolding revelation.

For myself, and for all people in our beautiful, yet wounded world, this is my prayer:

With God's grace,
may we always move forward together
    doing justice,
    loving goodness,
      and walking humbly with our God.

Philippians 1:9–10

"And this is my prayer:
that your love may increase
ever more and more in knowledge
and every kind of perception,
to discern what is of value…"

A MATTER OF VALUE

by **Martin Pable, OFM CAP**

O ver the years, this Scripture verse has guided and inspired me, both in my own spiritual journey and in my spiritual direction ministry with others. To consider its impact on my life and on the lives of those with whom I have ministered, first of all, let's recall the setting for these words of St. Paul.

He is in prison because he has been proclaiming the gospel of Jesus—his life and teachings and especially his death and resurrection. Philippi was a well-known city in northeastern Greece. According to the Acts of the Apostles (16:9–40), Paul had founded there the first Christian community in Europe. It seems it was one of his favorite communities. He had received news that the Christians there were growing in their faith, in their commitment to the gospel of Jesus, and in their care for one another. This brought him great comfort in his imprisonment.

In our text, after greeting the Philippians and assuring them of his love, he shares with them the focus of his own prayer: that their love "may increase ever more and more," and that they may "discern what is of value." Personally, I prefer the earlier (1970) translation from the *New American Bible*: "My prayer is that...*you may learn to value the things that really matter*." It seems to me that many of us (myself included) tend to place too much value (and spend too much time and energy) on things that do *not* really matter. I can become grossly agitated, for example, if I have to stop for two or more red lights while driving. I take it as a personal affront.

As you may recall, in the 1970s, educators were being encouraged to engage students in the exercise of "values clarification." Students were asked to write out what they personally considered to be important to strive for in life (not merely what parents or peers said). Educators were advised not to make any judgments on the students' choices, but merely to acknowledge them. There was surely benefit in this exercise, as it could lead to a deeper sense of self-awareness. The flaw, I believe, was in assuming that what the students *said* were their values were actually so. Values that are expressed at the verbal level are not necessarily lived out at the behavioral level.

In those days, I was both teaching and practicing pastoral counseling. It became evident that people were often unclear about what their true values were. Eventually, I came up with three criteria for discerning one's values. First, what do I spend *time* on? Second, what do I spend *money* on? And third, what do I spend *emotion* on? Regarding the last, what do I worry about? What do I get angry about? What do I get enthused about and rejoice over? What do I grieve over when it is missing? As people pondered these questions, they would come to a deeper self-awareness, which, in turn, allowed them to make changes in their behavior.

We have seen that St. Paul's prayer for his beloved Philippians is that "you may learn to value the things that really matter." Which in turn raises a key question—"What, then, really matters?" Does it really matter who wins the Academy Awards? Or the World Series? Or the Super Bowl? Does it matter if someone other than I gets credit or praise for the success of the parish festival? Or for the beautiful Christmas decorations in church? Does it really matter if I was not chosen as chair of the parish council or the Christian formation committee?

Getting back to Paul's Letter to the Philippians (1:12–18), Paul knows that he is in prison because of his preaching about Jesus. He knows that he now will be unable to continue his mission. And yet, he says, "my situation has turned out for the advancement of the gospel." Why? Because his imprisonment has emboldened others in the community to "proclaim the word fearlessly." Of course, he adds, some are doing this, "from envy and rivalry and selfish ambition, not from pure motives." But, so what, he says. "What difference does it make, as long as in every way, whether from specious motives or from genuine ones, Christ is being proclaimed? That is what brings me joy." This is the mature Paul, free now from self-concern, rivalry, and self-pity. He is concerned only that the Good News of Jesus is being proclaimed by the Christian community.

So, what really matters? That God is being honored and glorified through our lives of prayer and loving devotion. That the Good News of Jesus Christ is being proclaimed—his life, his teachings, and his healing ministry. The message that Jesus bestows mercy upon sinners, that he has compassion for those who are poor and hurting, is being spread. People are coming to know that Jesus was willing to suffer rejection, unjust accusation and condemnation, excruciating suffering, and a painful death. They learn that Jesus' resurrection and promise of eternal life for all who believe and follow him is real.

And for our own lives, what really matters is that we become wholehearted disciples of Jesus Christ. That we strive to grow in our personal relationship with him—through personal prayer, lifelong conversion through sharing in the sacraments of reconciliation and the Eucharist, and faithfully practicing the corporal and spiritual works of mercy. As St. Paul said so beautifully to his beloved Philippians:

> My prayer is that your love may more and
> more abound, both in understanding and
> wealth of experience, so that, with a clear
> conscience and blameless conduct, you may
> learn to value the things that really matter,
> up to the very day of Christ [the Final
> Judgment]. PHILIPPIANS 1:9–10

This perspective has helped me to be more at peace when things go wrong in my own life. When I get upset, frustrated, or angry, it helps to stop and ask myself: "Okay—how much does this really matter?" Most of the time I can honestly answer, "Not very much; in fact, very little." And from there I can move to, "Okay, then, let it go." And even if it is a serious matter, I know I can turn to God in prayer with confidence that he will help me move through it.

I've also learned something important about myself. If something goes wrong and it's somebody else's fault, I get upset momentarily. But it doesn't last long. But if it's something that was my own fault—I forgot something or neglected to follow through or did or said something that was hurtful—I have a difficult time letting it go. I tend to beat up on myself too much and for too long. I need to get better at forgiving myself once I admit my mistake and apologize.

In this regard, I have found great comfort in a verse from the lesser-known Old Testament prophet Micah. Speaking directly to God he says,

> Who is there like you, the God who removes
> guilt and pardons sin...; who does not persist
> in anger forever, but delights rather in
> clemency...? *You will cast into the depths of the*
> *sea all our sins.* MICAH 7:18–19

I have found those words comforting, not only for myself, but also for those who come to me for confession or spiritual direction. When they share with me some sin or serious mistake they have made, I ask if they have confessed it in the sacrament of reconciliation. If they say "Yes—I know God has forgiven me, but I can't forgive myself," I gently remind them that once we have repented of our sin or mistake and received absolution, the sin is gone—period. It's like God has a poor memory for our repented sins. Then I share with them the quote from Micah; and I add a line I once heard from a wise pastor: "And God puts a sign there that says, "NO FISHING!" In other words, "Don't keep going back into those waters!"

Such reminders can make a huge difference in one's life. And so, I ask you once again to recall those wonderful words of our brother, St. Paul: "My prayer is that your love may more and more abound [grow]...so that with a clear conscience and blameless conduct *you may learn to value the things that really matter*, up to the very day of Christ Jesus."

John 12:3

The house
was filled
with the fragrance
of the oil.

THE SCENT OF LOVE

by **Mary Marrocco**

Not accidentally, this Scripture verse showed up for me at a poignant moment in my life. I had fallen in love. It was just after I returned to graduate studies following five years of experience in pastoral work.

I'd had interests before—and heartbreaks—but nothing soul-stirring like this. This time, I knew some part of myself had been wakened to (painful) life. When I realized it, that part of me wanted to go get him and tell him immediately how I felt. Other parts of me clamored out in fear and alarm, holding me back.

Being a shy person, I was pretty good at loving from a distance—a habit that left me alone and uncertain. My friends were all getting on with their lives and relationships. There I was, angry with myself for not having the nerve to tell this man how I felt, yet shocked at myself for seriously considering doing so! He seemed far above me in all the ways that mattered. I was clearly unworthy, I felt, not to mention awkward and unseasoned. To top it off, he was already dating someone. They were on the verge of getting engaged. Surely I was breaking some code of honor by even thinking of him, let alone speaking to him about my thoughts. What if I told him how I felt and his reply was condescending? What if he was offended or merely amused? Or, worst of all, what if he felt sorry for me?

Safer to do nothing. Safer, and easier. But that strategy left me stuck and paralyzed. A powerful inner force was urging me forward even as much of me held back. Back and forth, thinking, analyzing, worrying, deciding and redeciding. It was torture, and I was the torturer. "What's wrong with me?" I asked myself. And, "What am I going to do about it?"

Sometimes, the seasons of our lives are in harmony with the seasons of the church. So it was in this case. My inner battle was played out on the purple fields of Lent. During several interminable weeks of indecision, my inner judge and I listened to the Lenten gospels with unprecedented attentiveness. And on the Fifth Sunday of Lent, I heard, as never before, the story of the woman anointing Jesus' feet with perfume (John 12:1–8, with parallels in Mark and Matthew).

Somehow, in my earlier thinking, the spotlight always seemed to be on the woman's wrongness and lowliness, with a condescension on Jesus' part, as he looked down on her kneeling at his feet and generously cancelled her deserved reprimand because she needed help. Now, my eyes were opened! I realized that this story is not like this at all. I had missed the core elements—the woman's profound desire for Christ, his love for her, and how such love changes everything!

Origen, back in the third century, taught that the Scriptures open themselves to us progressively, in ever-deepening layers. The more we love, study, live, and pray with them, the more they reveal to us. Like any relationship, our relationship with the Scriptures grows through time spent together. All at once, the fragrance of the woman's oil seemed to fill me and my house. A strong fragrance seemingly goes everywhere, inescapable, unless one were to cut off one's nose. Why, her scent was the scent of love! No wonder Jesus, the evangelists, and those present all found it so memorable (some of them found it memorably disgraceful).

I'd been listening to the gospel with my mind, with reason. Working on a graduate theology degree was a privilege, but I realized that it kept me too focused on the intellect. Suddenly, that was no longer enough. I needed to find the way of love. My body and all of my senses needed to be in on it, too. How had I overlooked it all these years?

That woman, washing Jesus' feet, was out of line, as people have known for two thousand years. She broke into a men's gathering and, uninvited, approached one of the guests and addressed him in an astonishingly intimate way, pouring scented oil on him. Thus, she usurped the role of the host, who would ordinarily perform such rites. Yet what she brought, what she did, who she was, smelled good. It beguiled the senses.

The sense of smell is powerful. Working with the homeless and outcast, I learned firsthand that some people don't smell good. That keeps others away from them. Dorrie, a woman who was a regular at the drop-in center where I volunteered, was generally alone for this reason. After her death, we learned that she was known to police as "the cat lady" because she kept a large number of cats in her little apartment and had taken on their scent as her own. Her loneliness and generosity offended our olfactory senses, but I am sure they were much more pleasantly fragrant to God.

Now that I had awakened and started smelling the perfume, I discovered with astonishment the gospel woman's courage. I also realized the challenge that she laid down. Here was I, keeping my heart hidden and protected, and there was she, so much more vulnerable than I, risking everything. She spent a year's salary on a bottle of oil, broke into the room on her own initiative, shattered the bottle so it could never be used again, and lavished the scent on Jesus' feet, keeping none back for other occasions. Nobody in the house could fail to be aware of this. There was nothing hidden about it.

"Show yourself!" she seemed to say to me; "show up! Take a risk because you want to be with Christ. Touch the real desire of your heart; admit that you love him and long to be with him. Go where you fear to go, where you do not belong, where others may judge, fear, and reject you! Let your true self be seen and heard and even smelled!" Belonging to Christ is personal, private, and sacred. It is also bold, public, and disturbing.

Now, this powerful Scripture passage was still speaking to me further. "You there, hiding in the corner," this brave woman seemed to continue, looking directly at me, "You are letting shame and fear keep you prisoner, mistaking them for friends. You can stay there forever and never know who you really are, or you can be bold, claim your love, and discover more than you ever dreamt."

"Well," I responded, "do you think my heart is important, then?"

I'd forgotten she was a "sinful" woman. To me, she was a real woman, alive in body and soul, and she was daring me to be alive that way, too. My love was love of a mere human. Hers was love of Christ. She seemed to think they were connected.

Much later, wandering in an art museum, I discovered a painting of this Scriptural scene. The depiction featured a sumptuous table, laden with all sorts of rich foods. Reclining all around the table were men equally rich in their dress. Jesus' head was with the men at table, but his feet were with the kneeling woman. He belonged to both, them and her. He physically connected them with each other, whether they liked it or not.

Jesus unites. People come to him who would never choose each other. And that brings them together. And changes them, if they let it. Change, at the deepest level, is possible, even in places that seem absolutely immovable. The woman was changed by Christ's love. Therefore, she changed her life. In turn, her life changed the community to which she did not belong, but which she entered because, through Christ, she did belong. Love is never for oneself alone. Love belongs to all, and affects all.

Christ unites: rich with poor, man with woman, righteous with sinner, neighbor with neighbor, human with divine, body with soul. He receives the woman's gifts, letting her ointment and hair flow over his skin. Christ, "well in his skin," is not distressed by her touch. How could he be? He is God's love made visible and touchable. He is the Sacrament that gives us the sacraments.

Just after Easter, I took the risk. And the man, to whom I had previously been so afraid to even speak, echoed my feelings! We talked for a long time, an experience that was real and clear like a mountain stream. I would never have known that response had I not trusted my heart. It was surprisingly simple and profoundly beautiful.

In the end, he didn't change his life to be with me. But more importantly (as it turned out), my life was changed. Through "daring" for love, through risking the suffering that came with it, I found myself at Jesus' feet. It wasn't about learning to love that particular man, after all. It was about learning to love.

I can't say that since then I've never held back in fear, shame, doubt, envy, or the many other afflictions of the human heart. But I had discovered a new way, not just in thought, but in the flesh and in action. Did that happen for her when she broke in and disturbed everything?

How did the woman with the questionable etiquette come to know what the respectable men eating with Jesus were oblivious to? The woman's broken bottle spilled out fragrance and balm. The broken places in the heart are the ones that let in light and peace, giving us the courage to reach out to others in ways we never could otherwise. Broken, poured out, given, received; this is the secret of love. She gives it all, and more. She mirrors the measureless, overflowing love of God. We give carefully. God gives totally and, (seemingly) fool-ishly, like someone madly in love.

All three gospels tell us that this encounter hap-pened in Bethany. John's gospel tells us that the home was that of Lazarus, telling us further that it was Lazarus' sister, Mary, who entered so memorably and took her place at the feet of Jesus, anointing them, doing what she always did, what she was born to do.

Jesus sees the meaning of her gesture. His compan-ions do not. All the evangelists record that some men were disturbed by the woman's exuberant act. Blind to what happened before their eyes, they focused on money. The oil could have been sold and the money could have been given to the poor, they protested. Jesus, who, "did not need anyone to testify about human nature; he himself understood it well" (John 2:25), sees through their self-deception, something that I can now recognize too. If I am sparing in my love of Christ, it is not out of love for the poor; to love Christ is to love the poor.

John's gospel tells us this anointing happened six days before Passover, which means just a week before Jesus' death. Touching him that day, Mary anointed in advance the body that was about to be broken and buried. She touched the power of life, stronger after all than the power of death.

Ever since that memorable year, now when I am feeling bound by fear, shame, or doubt, the scent of her fragrant oil breaks my bonds and helps me go free. Jesus foretold that, wherever the Good News is proclaimed, what this woman did would be remembered and told. It has been.

Psalm 51:3

Have mercy on me, God,
in accord with your merciful love;
in your abundant compassion
blot out my transgressions.

ABUNDANT COMPASSION, DIMINISHING FEAR

by **Mark Neilsen**

One morning I came upon a slick red car with all its windows shot out, looking like a skeleton on wheels in front of the apartment building two doors down. Reportedly, its owner had made the mistake of selling drugs on a rival's turf. The neighborhood had its rough spots, but nothing so dramatic as this, so close to my home, my wife, and our three children under the age of ten. Though I was trying to follow God's will, at that moment everything seemed to be coming apart, including the fragile faith I had rediscovered.

I left the church easily in college after yielding to doubts in the resurrection and other tenets of faith. No longer constrained by the commandments and untethered to any spiritual or moral anchor, I could drift freely in the counterculture of the 1960s. For a while, that was great fun.

But over the months and years, trying to shape one's own moral order and understanding of the universe—things provided by the church and other mainstream institutions—became a wearisome full-time job. Particularly so after I had left graduate school for a second and final time, broken up with my girlfriend, and foundered without a direction for my life. At a low point, I wondered if I would, as my father had, succumb to a crippling depression. Though it was doing me no good, atheism seemed inescapable at the time—until one morning when it didn't.

Lying in bed, not intentionally praying or seeking a religious answer to my distress, I threw a question out to the universe—and an answer came back, assuring me that there was a solid truth about life on which one could rely. I didn't instantly become a believer, much less return to the church, but I suddenly had the sense that there did exist a spiritual light, and if I directed my steps toward it, all would be well.

A few weeks later, I opted for a new start, moving from Milwaukee to St. Louis, a city where a friend from college was going to graduate school. I gradually found myself drawn back to the church via a group of lay men and women living in a faith-based community, and before long I joined them, one of whom I would eventually marry.

By small degrees, a new life began to take shape, based on an ideal of Christian simplicity and solidarity with the poor. Not that anyone would have then confused me with Dorothy Day or Mother Teresa, but they along with Thomas Merton became guides, proofs that religion didn't have to be small, stifling, or joyless. In an atmosphere of hope and friendship, my spirits began to revive.

Years later, still living in community of about a dozen people, I was facing several challenges that were not easily resolved. Our commitment to live and own property in a low-income, racially integrated urban neighborhood was being tested in the late 1980s when the area began to feel the impact of crack cocaine and spreading gang violence. We put down roots, made friends with some of our neighbors, became involved in local politics, and attended the local parish. But now that stability was threatened.

At home, our marriage was strong and I loved being a father, but I was learning that the responsibilities of parenting went beyond changing diapers and comforting a crying child in the night. My wife and I took part-time jobs, she as a nurse in a nearby hospital and I as a writer of newsletters for the Human Rights Office of the archdiocese, so that each of us could be involved in the raising of the kids.

Entrusted with the care of our children, we began to consider things like life insurance, wills, and the custody of our children should we suddenly die. These questions were complicated by the fact that part of our community's radical vision involved sharing income and property through an informal arrangement subject to adaptation over time. But concrete financial questions about the future, especially involving the children, seemed to me to require a similarly concrete structure.

Change is seldom easy, and the experiment with a new paradigm of lay men and women living in a community based on faith, social justice, and simplicity was attractive and powerful. But reaching consensus became difficult as fissures emerged despite good will.

We spent hours and hours over the course of several years in community meetings trying to fashion a new financial arrangement that could satisfy everyone's needs. Radical sharing had been a foundational value for the community, and the idea of letting it go was unsettling to our collective identity.

As our twin sons approached first grade at the same school as their older sister, my wife and I agreed this would be a good time for me to look for a full-time position as a writer. That, however, meant a major shift of vocation: from direct involvement in the church's social justice mission to immersion in the for-profit world of publishing.

Meanwhile, my mother, who was living three hundred miles away, began to exhibit symptoms of Alzheimer's disease, requiring more attention from my siblings and me and finally leading us to make the difficult decision to place her in a nursing home. At age fifteen I had suddenly lost my father to suicide; now I was gradually losing my mother.

The tensions of those days came to a head one morning a few days after the shooting out of the car windows. I was helping a friend install new kitchen cabinets in our home, an exercise that seemed futile, given the fragility of the neighborhood and our living situation. I needed to drive to the hardware store for some extra supplies, and on the way, my anguish and fear roiled up to the point that I wondered if the devil himself were somehow an intimate actor in the situation. Were the decisions I was making carrying me further and further away from the merciful God I had been trying to follow?

I began to shake, fearful that my life was spinning out of control, even as it had years earlier when I was unbelieving. I felt in grave danger of losing everything good that had come my way in the intervening years. Having tried to figure out what was right in God's eyes and avoid the mistakes of the past, I seemed to be once again stuck trying to find a safe and moral place to stand. As it turned out, I desperately needed the grace of God, something I could never fashion for myself, no matter how carefully I tried to think and act correctly.

Here's how I described in my journal what happened next:

Immediately I called upon the name of
Jesus and spontaneously this prayer formed
in my mind: "Lord Jesus Christ, from your
abundant mercy cast out my fear." Instantly
I felt increasing calm and confidence, so I
repeated it like a mantra, emphasizing the
last four words. Sometimes I would say,
"Lord Jesus Christ in your abundant mercy,
cast out my sin." This latter made sense,
for there have been many sins to which I've
clung, even though I don't think [my] fear is a
punishment for being a sinner.

The inner turmoil didn't instantly go away, but it did
diminish dramatically. I began to rely on this and other
similar verses of Scripture in moments of spontaneous
prayer. Little by little, I began to see that I didn't have
to get things right, that God wouldn't abandon me if
I made a mistake or decided to set out on a new path.

My attitude about problems slowly softened. In the
midst of neighborhood chaos, I began to pray, "Lord,
if you want me to stay here, make that possible for
me. If you want me to leave, show me a path forward."
Gradually, I began to trust more in God's presence and
action in my life.

Ultimately, we divided up our communally held property among the households, and before long formal community was gradually replaced by the bonds of friendship. We have stayed in the neighborhood, which has stabilized in recent years, though the challenges of urban living remain.

Not as fearful as in the past, I still worry too much about being right and, even in trivial situations, have a hard time letting go of what I can't control. Probably too individualistic to have ever thrived in close community, I struggle when I am out of step with others and risk their disapproval. But these days, I am more confident than ever that God desires our freedom from oppression of any kind. When mistakes or weakness threaten to plunge me into despair, the words of Scripture are always there to remind me of God's abundant mercy and compassion.

Matthew 6:26, 28

"Look at the
birds in the sky...
Learn from the way
the wildflowers grow."

NATURAL, SACRED REMINDERS

by **Melannie Svoboda, SND**

One day, Jesus was standing outside on the side of a hill. A large crowd gathered around him eager to hear him speak. Among the things he said that day were these words: "Look at the birds in the sky... Learn from the way the wildflowers grow." These simple words are among my favorite words of Jesus. Why? Because I see in them three important directives for living my Christian faith, directives I need to be reminded of regularly: Trust in God, maintain a contemplative attitude toward life, and view creation as sacred.

Trust in God. In order to appreciate this first implication of Jesus' words, I think it's important to know the context in which they were spoken. As I said, Jesus spoke these words outside, not inside of a synagogue or other building. Consequently, the birds and wildflowers were probably visible to him and to his audience. Jesus begins his preaching with these words: "Do not worry." In the course of this discourse, he says these words not once, but three times. Then he offers an alternative to worry: Trust in God. Why should we trust in God? We trust in God, Jesus says, because the God who loves and cares for the birds and the wildflowers loves and cares for us even more. This deep and unwavering love of God will provide for all we need on our life's journey.

This lesson about trusting in God is especially important for me because I tend to worry about things. Maybe you do too. I worry about BIG things like the global economy, world peace, the environment, a potential nuclear disaster. And I worry about things closer to home like my loved ones, work, personal relationships, and health issues. Sometimes, I even fret over smaller matters and I ask myself, *Will it rain on my picnic?* Or, *Will my soufflé collapse?* The human propensity to worry is illustrated in the cartoon strip *Peanuts.* One day Charlie Brown confesses to Linus, "I worry about school a lot." Then he adds, "I worry about my worrying so much about school." And finally, he says, "Even my anxieties have anxieties!"

Jesus understands human anxiety, so he offers us some good reasons to not worry. For one thing, worry is not productive. It is actually useless. We cannot "add a single moment" to our life span by worrying, Jesus says. Worry can also upset and distract us from what's really important in life. After all, we are to "seek first the kingdom of God."

In *The Little Book of Letting Go*, Hugh Prather says that worry "fragments the mind, shatters focus, distorts perspective, and destroys inner peace." Surely, Jesus does not desire his disciples to be saddled with such side effects. Elsewhere in the gospel, Jesus tells his disciples many times to "fear not," to "have peace," and even to "come aside and rest awhile." We can do none of those things if we are always fretting about something.

Many times, I have been inspired by the deep trust in God I have witnessed in others. For example, my sister, Mary Ann. One year, the day before Thanksgiving, she was told she had cancer in her stomach, liver, and kidneys. The first words out of her mouth were, "It's all in God's hands." What a beautiful example of Christian faith! My sister, (not coincidentally) loved birds, especially cardinals, and she loved flowers, especially daisies. She always kept bird feeders and flowers on her apartment balcony. As I journey through life, I try to notice the birds and the flowers every day. When I am tempted to worry or fret over something, they become gentle reminders to me that the whole world is, indeed, in God's hands.

The second directive is to *Maintain a contemplative attitude toward life*. Jesus tells us to *look at* and to *learn from* the birds and the wildflowers. Other translations say *notice*, *observe*, *think about*, and *consider*. For me, these words describe a contemplative attitude toward life. Jesus is warning us not to live our lives thoughtlessly or superficially. He tells us instead to pay attention to the world around us. He asks us to take time to reflect on our experiences—just as he did. How can we nurture this contemplative attitude toward life? I think that the best way to begin is to simply slow down. After all, we don't notice things if we are always in a rush. Barbara Brown Taylor, in her book *Altar in the World*, writes: "Most of us move so quickly that our surroundings become no more than the blurred scenery we fly past on our way to somewhere else." To prevent such haste, I try to walk less hurriedly, eat less quickly, and drive less frantically.

Once we begin to slow down, we find that we are more apt to notice the people in our lives—*really* notice them. This noticing will help us to interact with them more respectfully and meaningfully. We might also consider the circumstances of our lives and decide if we need to make some changes. Additionally, we will be better prepared to reflect on our thoughts and feelings in order to detect the movement of God's Spirit. Finally, slowing down can help us to notice individuals who are in need and to take some action on their behalf.

For me, the words *notice*, *consider*, and *think about* are really a call to prayer. Sometimes, I'm tempted to think I'm too busy to pray. After all, I have community and family obligations, writing deadlines, and talks and retreats to prepare. But then I recall the example of

Jesus. He was a very busy man, yet he regularly took time to go off by himself to pray. Our prayer can take many forms: reciting the psalms, saying the Rosary, dialoging with Jesus, reflecting on the readings of the day, sitting before the Blessed Sacrament, reading a spiritual book (such as this one), jotting in a journal, or simply sitting in silence.

Why do we need prayer in our daily lives? Because prayer gives us strength to face life's many challenges. I like what Dorothy Day said about her prayer: "My strength returns to me with my morning cup of coffee and reading the psalms." Henri Nouwen said that, without daily prayer, his life "loses its coherency and I start experiencing my day as a series of random incidents and accidents." Ultimately, we pray not because we love prayer, but because we love God. Nourishing that loving relationship with God is the most important thing I do in my life. This doesn't mean that prayer has to be a chore. Remember the advice Thomas Merton gave to a friend: "Quit trying so hard in prayer," he said. "How does an apple ripen? It just sits in the sun."

Third, I *view creation as sacred*. Jesus points to the birds and flowers. This simple gesture demonstrates one of his most notable characteristics—he was close to nature. More than that, he loved nature and drew spiritual nourishment from the natural world. Incorporating nature into his teachings, Jesus speaks about natural phenomena such as mustard seeds, grapevines, grains of wheat, fig trees, and even weeds. His preaching features a variety of animals such as sheep, goats, mother hens, camels, snakes, donkeys, foxes, doves, and wolves. Jesus is well acquainted with various natural processes too, speaking of yeast causing dough to rise, grapes fermenting into fine wine, a woman giving birth, clouds bringing much needed rain, and fertilizer enriching the soil.

Jesus even identifies himself and his teaching with natural elements. Water, light, fire, and wind are all featured. He calls his first apostles, not while walking in the temple, but while strolling along the shore of the Sea of Galilee. In the early morning hours, he goes up into the hills to pray. And the night he is arrested, where do Judas and the Roman soldiers find him? That's right, in a garden called Gethsemane where he is seeking solace and strength amid the gnarled olive trees. For Jesus, the world of the divine intertwines with the "ordinary" of nature. He teaches us that creation itself is a kind of Divine Revelation.

"If you have an eye for it, the world itself is a sacrament," St. Augustine wrote over 1,600 years ago. Jesus possessed this sacramental view of the world. It is a view we, his followers, desperately need to reclaim today. And we have help. Pope Francis wrote an entire encyclical, *Laudato Si'*, on the sacredness of the natural world and our relationship with it. This encyclical mirrors thoughts and attitudes that can be traced all the way back to Jesus' teaching on that hillside. Pope Francis wrote, "The entire material universe speaks of God's love, his boundless affection for us. Soil, water, mountains, everything is, as it were, a caress of God" (no. 84). And we might add, "So are birds and wildflowers!"

The Holy Father went on to say, "The universe unfolds in God, who fills it completely. Hence, there is a mystical meaning to be found in a leaf, in a mountain trail, in a dew drop, in a person's face" (no. 223). Pope Francis also challenges us saying, "Christians need an ecological conversion, whereby the effects of their encounter with Jesus Christ become evident in their relationship to the world around them" (no. 217). In other words, care for our environment is an integral part of being a follower of Jesus.

Birds and wildflowers—visible reminders of God's great love and care for us. *Notice, observe, consider, pray*—directives for a contemplative attitude toward life. *Nature as sacred*—Creation as Divine Revelation. That's why these words of Jesus mean so much to me.

Genesis 50:20

Even though you
meant harm to me,
God meant it for good,
to achieve this present
end, the survival of
many people.

THE BEST THING THAT EVER HAPPENED

by Amy Welborn

My friend Molly had been battling various forms of cancer for many years. Now, it seemed, the cancer was winning, and Molly, about ten years older than I, had months or perhaps even weeks to live.

I had moved to another state, but when I heard this news, I traveled to Florida one September weekend to see my friend. I had taught her children; she had taught mine. But that was years ago, and now we sat in the living room of her bungalow, and she told me what it felt like to watch your physical life slip away.

"Soon, I won't be able to walk," she observed, pointing to her stick-thin, yellowing legs.

When she was first diagnosed she had vowed to stay alive "because I want to see grandchildren"—and now she had four. She was a little frightened, she said, and was sad to leave "this beautiful world and this beautiful life," but she had faith in God's promise of something even more beautiful.

And then she said something startling. She said, "I'm glad I got cancer. It was the best thing that ever happened to me."

She continued, saying that before her diagnosis, she had been vain and superficial. Now, I had known Molly before cancer struck, and even then, I would have described her as one of the most deeply spiritual people I had ever known. But at that moment, I had to trust her self-understanding.

"I didn't really appreciate the gift of life—*at all*—before I got cancer," she said.

About a month later, eight months to the day after my own husband had died suddenly from a heart attack, Molly "went peacefully home," as her daughter wrote. It was also the feast of St. Francis, the suffering *poverello* who praised God, in his *Canticle*, for Sister Death, through whom the blessed meet God.

Molly's daughter, who sent me the news of her mother's passing, had her own story. She had married right out of college and soon had a baby girl. When that baby was four months old, eight years before her mother died, Nancy's husband was killed in a car accident.

A couple of years later, Nancy remarried, and a year after that, she gave birth to another child.

She was happy, she said, but it was all still a mystery, this dance of life and death. If her first husband had not been tragically killed, her younger child would not exist.

This mystery, embodied in a single family's suffering and joy, never fails to stop me in my tracks. I know that if I could examine my own family history in detail, what I would see is such a strange, truly inscrutable tapestry that led to me being here, right now.

There would be accidents. There would be conscious, joyful intention. There would be a missed train that resulted in a chance meeting that ended up in a marriage. There might be an argument over something meaningless or something vital, an argument that was settled, which led to intimacy that led to a great-great-great grandparent. There would be great movements of people and wars in which my ancestors were caught up, their lives transformed. There would be small movements across town, a choice to go to this college and not that one, a cough correctly diagnosed, a strange ache ignored. Encounters, choices, missteps, and yes, outright evil.

And here I am. Here you are. Who can make sense of it all? Where is the logic in it?

Joseph, of course, was the victim of wrongdoing. His jealous brothers sold him into slavery, then lied to their father about it all. This could have been the end of Joseph, but the same gifts that irritated his brothers to the point of deep sin rescued him. He interpreted dreams, and he used what was revealed to him to save, not only himself, but thousands of others.

Years later, his brothers arrived in Egypt, seeking food for those afflicted by famine. As they came to understand that the man in control of the resources, and therefore their future, was indeed the brother against whom they had sinned, they were naturally fearful, and even more so later, when their father and protector, Jacob, died. They were convinced that they would be defenseless against any wrath, any vengeance, and they knew it was deserved.

But Joseph's interaction with the transcendent and real did not stop with dreams. He understood that God's ways are not our ways. It was a terrible thing his brothers had done. He had suffered a great deal from their actions, as had others, including their father Jacob. But God is stronger than our most evil intentions. He can use anything and all that we do and, in his mercy and power, bring good out of it.

So, because Joseph was where he was when he was—even if evil choices had sent him there—good happened because of it. Lives were saved.

When I contemplate the strange trajectory of my family history and even my own time on earth so far, I am comforted by Joseph's words to his brothers. They aren't, I hasten to add, an invitation to magical or simplistic thinking. I'm not a fan of talking about "God's plan," which seems to diminish God's responsiveness and creativity. No, keeping Joseph's words at the heart of my life means that I know that woven through this tapestry that is the paradigm of my life are two complementary strands: God's powerful love and my free will to welcome it.

For you notice that Joseph was not passive. As the victim of various evil acts, he didn't just sit back and say, "God's got this" and do nothing. He vigorously and unfailingly continued to use the gifts God had given him. He was certainly a victim, but he didn't play the victim. God turned the evil Joseph suffered to good—with Joseph's help and with his cooperation.

So I consider my own life. Mine differs from yours in the particulars, but not, I'd imagine, in the general shape of it: that mix of good and ill I described in the beginning. Parents in a difficult marriage, a household marked by tension, drinking, and anger. No siblings, which children of large families might envy, but trust me—don't. Naïveté of young adulthood that led to exploitation and mistreatment, leaving me vulnerable to a terribly ill-conceived early marriage. Wanderings along the way, a happy second marriage that ended one morning when a fifty-year-old man dropped dead on a treadmill at a local YMCA.

So what will I do with it? What will I make of it, the good and the bad? Will I choose to be a victim, or will I follow Joseph's lead and dig deeply, not give up, and let God use whatever I have, wherever I am, to do good?

To be a more open, honest, and accepting parent? To take my own issues to prayer and professional help and not let them be a burden to others in my care, to not make them victims of my stuff? To be aware of my family history with alcohol and raise my children with that awareness? To always, always keep the lines of communication open so my kids *always* know that there is someone completely on their side whom they can approach and tell *anything*?

To help my sons who are growing up without their father—boys whom I cannot believe with my very human brain and heart are better off without their father than they would be if he was still alive—to help them live with this hole in their lives, to accept it, and to seek to fill that gap with God's love, and nothing less?

No one tossed me into a pit or sold me into slavery. I know many, many people who have suffered more than I have. So no, it's not the worst, by any means, but neither anything anyone would plan, if they could sketch out the life they'd like to lead.

But this is it. This is my life, the life God so graciously gave me, and how can I not awaken every morning and say *Thank you*?

For God has indeed brought good out of even the minor suffering I've endured in this life. He has brought children, and yes, when I consider their lives and the odd and even harmful circumstances that led to their existence, I am moved to dig very deeply and consider the real shape of gratitude. Can I be grateful to God even for those circumstances that caused me great suffering—because I know that if I hadn't been in those places at those times, these human beings, now on their own paths, wouldn't exist? Can I, like Molly, look at what the world sees as tragedy and say: *"That was the best thing that ever happened to me"*?

I take a deep breath, and say yes. I can and I must be grateful, and Joseph's words to his brothers are the way I articulate that gratitude. They are words of comfort. They help me guard against despair. They are an anchor of meaning and purpose in a world that seems ruled by randomness. They are a spur to humility. And finally, they are a reminder to never be passive and unrealistic: I am here, God is here, and with his help, I can see where I am called to go next, in trust, love, and hope.

Matthew 25:40

"Amen, I say to you,
whatever you did for one
of the least brothers
of mine, you did for me."

IF I HAD KNOWN
IT WAS YOU...

by **Steve Givens**

I first became enthralled by this verse as a teenager watching the movie version of the musical *Godspell*. As the character of Jesus tells this parable of the final judgment and separates the sheep from the goats (his disciples down on all fours baa-ing and looking lost), my eyes were fixed on those poor goats. They were being directed to the left because they had failed to recognize Jesus in their encounters with those in need. Taken aback by this command to love even the strangers among us, one of them says to Jesus in a sultry voice, "If we'd known it was you, we'd have taken you around the corner for a cup of coffee!" And that, for me, became a lifetime challenge. "Well, of course if I'd known it was you, Jesus...!"

Admittedly, when I first began to let these verses sink in, I was focused not on verse 40 but on the very similar verse that ends the parable in verse 45: "Amen, I say to you, what you did *not* do for one of these least ones, you did *not* do for me." There's a big difference between those two verses, even though they differ by just a few words. I was worried about what I might not do or recognize. I was afraid of being the goat during the final judgment. I was more concerned about letting Jesus down than I was encouraged to serve others. The idea frightened me and the story stuck with me.

Until that point in my life, I had a deeply ingrained belief that my faith was just about me and God. Faith alone. I had been taught the Golden Rule and to be kind to others, but my young brain and fledgling spirit had not made the jump between believing in Jesus and caring for those around me in any substantial way. Perhaps it was my adolescent understanding of the relationship between faith and works. Perhaps I just didn't want to be bothered. I knew from my religious upbringing that I needed Jesus and I needed faith. Caring for others was nice, but not required, I thought.

My perspective began to shift when I was about eighteen. I received a call from a Marianist brother at a local retreat center. The river that flowed near the center had flooded its banks and, although the center was safe on its hill, the small community on the flat-land near the river had been devastated. Could I come help with the clean up? I arrived early on a Saturday morning and found families in tears, sorting through their meager possessions and rinsing the mud from their clothes, their furniture, their lives. I grabbed a shovel and did what I could. I looked in the faces of the newly homeless and thought of the parable. "Help me," Jesus was saying to me.

My understanding of the story of sheep and goats deepened and widened as time went on. My appreciation of the interconnectedness of faith and the care for others began to shift and evolve—a movement from fear to love.

Seeing Jesus in "the least of these" became less a foreboding and forewarning of standing before Jesus to be judged, and more the starting point for my understanding of human love, charity, everyday kindness, and justice. I began to grow and to look for opportunities to serve.

A few years after my experience with the flood victims, I was volunteering in the women's section of a local prison. I was trying to be Christ and to see Christ in the midst of the hopelessness of these women. One Saturday, I facilitated a discussion about the importance of faith as the basis for hope. One woman sat with her eyes downcast, never looking up as other women joined in the conversation, telling their personal stories of hope, both lost and found. Finally, as I was about to wrap up the conversation, she raised her head and said, "I think that's what happened to me—I just lost hope." In that moment, we all saw not a woman who had murdered her three young daughters, but the face of Christ. "Understand me," Jesus said to me.

Jesus' parable reflects the "mitzvah of hospitality" as found in Isaiah, chapter 58, outlining for us the corporal works of mercy, the care and feeding of the lives and bodies of those around us. Jesus certainly knew what was written in Isaiah and was teaching his followers what he had learned from childhood—feed the hungry, give water to the thirsty, clothe the naked, shelter the homeless, visit the sick, visit the imprisoned, and bury the dead.

Matthew 25 has led me to at least try to understand what it means to be the other and the outcast. It nudged me into parishes rich and poor. It "sent me" into soup kitchens, hospitals, hospices, prisons, and foreign missions. Matthew 25 inspired me to give financially to organizations that do this work daily. Most importantly, it allowed me to see the world and those in it through a different set of eyes. I was able to move from, "I wonder what they did (or didn't do) to get in that position," to, "that could be Jesus right in front of me, there on the street corner begging for coins."

So, instead of sidestepping the nameless guy who panhandles near the university where I work, I approached him and smiled. I asked him his name and looked him in the eye. His name is Keith. It turns out that he grew up about a mile from where I did. We're about the same age. I got some breaks that he didn't. I wish he could move on and get off the streets. "Don't judge me," Jesus said to me.

I started to see the world and its problems not as the result of people's faults, actions, and inactions, but as vast and great opportunities to practice charity and, ultimately and more importantly, to work for justice. For both charity and justice are necessary as we take up the corporal works of mercy. We must be willing to roll up our sleeves and help those in desperate need. And we must be willing to seek justice and social change by working to eradicate the root causes of those problems.

I have learned—with this Scripture coursing through my veins—that my response to those in need must stem not from pity, but from the deep understanding that the difference between "us" and "them" is a very fine line. My life could have been flooded away, had I lived someplace different. I could have been sitting in prison, speaking of lost hope. Keith and I lived a mile apart forty years ago. What if our addresses and our races had been swapped? Where would I be standing today?

Living Matthew 25 means finding the truth in the old saying, "There but for the grace of God go I." I began to understand that I stood where I stood—safe, warm, healthy, and free—not because I was better than anyone else, but perhaps only because I was born in the right place at a better time. I was living my life by the luck of geography and DNA. My existence had everything to do with God and the free gift I had been given. Because of all that, I had a responsibility to live my life faithfully and compassionately. I was, and am, responsible for caring for those around me whose life circumstances dictated that they walk a different and more difficult path.

About ten years ago, I faced my own moment of "poverty" when I was diagnosed with a rare blood disease and underwent three years of chemotherapy. In those dark days, I had the opportunity to be the one on the receiving end of care. Weakened by the disease and the treatment, I needed to let others "wash my feet." It was humbling and not always comfortable. I made a note to remember that. When I made it through (I'm about six years in remission now), I volunteered with a local hospice and learned to just sit and listen to the stories of those approaching death. They didn't need my wisdom or pity. They just needed someone to listen, to see in their faces more than their impending death. "Listen to me," Jesus said to me.

All this is not to say that I have always lived up to this lofty ideal. Many a year went by when I was too lazy or too immersed in my own world to get up out of bed on a Saturday or Sunday morning and head to the prison or to the hospital. Many times, I looked away so

I didn't have to witness what I didn't want to see. But a seed had been sown by this story, And from it grew something that would not easily go away. Somewhere deep there was always a tugging on my heart, always a quiet voice that whispered, "What if it's Jesus you're ignoring?"

To see Jesus in the faces of those in need is to have our lives transformed by the power of love. To serve the homeless is to embrace the poverty and humanity of the Incarnate Word of God. To care for the sick, injured, and diseased is to bind up the wounds of the crucified, bleeding, hurting, and human Jesus. To visit the lonely and imprisoned is to walk the way to Golgotha with Jesus, to shoulder the cross for even a few steps and hear the sound of metal on metal and the cries of his mother.

To recognize and embrace the broken in the world is to see Jesus and cling to him. The parable of the sheep and the goats in Matthew 25 is perhaps the great and lasting challenge of our lives. For it is, above all, about loving Christ, loving as Christ loved, and loving others as though they were Christ, all at the same time. "Love me," Jesus says to us all.

John 15:4

"Remain in me,
as I remain
in you."

MAKE YOURSELF
AT HOME

by Patricia Livingston

"I t changed my life," people are often quoted as saying about things from winning the lottery to falling in love. When I was invited to contribute a chapter to this book on life-changing Scripture verses, one verse came to my mind: John 15:4. It gave me great love and a wealth of spiritual realization at the same time.

The verb in this verse is the Greek word *meno*. It has a meaning that can be translated in English as "remain in," "abide in," or, in the translation in which I first read it, as "make your home in." In the *Jerusalem Bible* (1966), John 15:4 is translated: "Make your home in me as I make mine in you."

The life-changing aspect of the verse is that it freed me to let go of how I had once understood my relationship with God and God's with me. I grew up with a very strict Army officer father who returned from World War II probably suffering from what we now describe as post-traumatic stress syndrome. Punishment for not keeping the rules, not getting a good report card, saying anything that could be construed as "answering back," was immediate.

In my parochial grade school, the teaching on sin was frightening for me. If you sinned even a little and died, you would burn in Purgatory until you paid for it.

If you died in mortal sin, you would be in agony in hell forever. We were lined up every Friday to go to confession and ask for forgiveness.

My image of God, although not of a terrifying tyrant, was still someone distant, all-powerful, and all-knowing, whom I needed to work hard to keep rules to please. Even the term "all-loving" from the catechism made loving seem like a remote abstraction.

As the years went by I experienced other religious education and spiritual practices, and, in the new worlds of marriage and motherhood, my understanding of life was greatly expanded. In my relationship to God, I still felt a sense of duty, but there was More, a more I did not have language to describe.

Then, after thirteen years, the marriage ended in divorce. I was thrown into the psychological wilderness that is powerfully portrayed in the musical *Into the Woods*. I was lost in the forest of the unknown, trying to find my way, trying to make sense of what was left of what I had hoped and expected.

It was at this time, after weeks of wandering in the dark, that I came across John 15:4 in my *Jerusalem Bible*. I heard it as if I had never heard it before. "Make your home in me, as I make mine in you."

With my actual home with my daughter and two sons so changed by their father's leaving, I had been struggling with the whole concept of home. This Scripture verse inviting me to be home in God felt as if Love held its arms out.

Even more astounding than my being invited to make my home in God was the stated fact that God had already made God's home in me. God at home, here, now, in me! It was not up to me to make it happen. God was already at home. I just needed to realize that and to respond by making myself at home. So far from being asked to appear before a judge or bow down before a king, I was invited to enter and rest in the shelter of love.

What began then for me, and has continued through the many chapters and seasons since, was exploring the meaning of home. I went back in my memory to times and places where I had felt at home. I tried to name something I had experienced then that could be true of being home in God.

Three memories from my girlhood illustrated for me central features of what being home in God could mean. The first was a sense of being safe and loved despite real threat. My first home was with my mother's parents on Main Street in a small New Jersey town while my father was away in the army in World War II. Very vivid for me in those earliest memories was a feeling of being deeply welcomed, lovingly held. Even though Mom and Grandma and Grandpa sometimes spoke in stark whispers, turning down the radio news if they saw we were listening, I felt safe in their love. I remember the security of falling asleep to the sound of Grandpa's snoring down the hall. I was not alone.

Every loving aspect of the memory of those years is key for me to being at home in God. The sense of being held in welcome love turns down the volume on threats broadcast from the chaos that erupts in daily living.

The second feature of home, I realized looking back, is one I can only describe as a kind of gentle coziness. A kind of relaxed, lighthearted warmth. It is the quality that was contained in a second early memory where I had a sense of home even in a very improbable setting. My father was ordered to join General MacArthur's Headquarters Staff in Tokyo at the beginning of the occupation of Japan at the end of the war. Mom was told to join him soon afterward with us. (By then we were three girls — I am the middle.)

We lived in three different places in Tokyo, each time moved to what was considered a more secure location as the Korean War raged. By this time I was much more aware of danger than I had been. What I remember is something special that helped me feel safe. In each place we lived, in the corner of our closet, my sisters and I made what we called "a house in the silk blanket." The "silk blanket" was an old double-bed quilt Mom let us play with that we would somehow fold and prop up so we could all three fit into it with our dolls and library books.

Something that really touched me when I remembered it was that our favorite book was one my older sister Peggy read aloud to us over and over. It was called *The Little House in the Big Woods* by Laura Ingalls Wilder. As the Ingalls family had sheltered in their log cabin in the woods, we felt snugly safe in our house in the silk blanket in the corner of the closet.

This memory contributed a precious comfortable aspect of my sense of being at home in God. I was delighted to have that affirmed once by Bishop Kenneth Untener of Saginaw, Michigan, when I heard him translate the word *meno* in John 15:4 as God's invitation to "settle in for a while and relax."

This aspect of being at home as a chance to let go and relax is vivid for me so often when I walk through my front door, out of the rain, out of the traffic, finally home from a trip. I treasure knowing my oneness with God can have the same warm ease.

A third light on the verse from an early memory happened just after our getting off the boat in San Francisco when we came back from Tokyo. Suddenly

I realized with astonishment and delight that I could read the signs! They were in English! The first big billboard was an advertisement for a restaurant. Being able to read the language of God's signs is at the heart of making God home, and being fed by the food of love.

The bedrock of my spirituality is trying to pay attention to God's signs of present love, which I believe are any kind of goodness in the present moment. Noticing that goodness, pausing to take a deep grateful breath, is, for me, like walking through the doorway. Right here—now—I am home in God.

It keeps me centered as weeks unfold and has been the saving grace in crises—when my grandson was shot, when my daughter's house burned, when my husband was diagnosed with advanced cancer. (I married again after twenty years.)

Every day, when I slow myself to be mindful, I experience goodness poured out in love—from the intimacy of the Eucharist to kindness from a stranger. There is the first taste of morning coffee, some texted pictures from a grandchild, a tiny moon shining in the night sky, curved exactly like a smile. Every evening my husband and I give thanks as we share a goodness story from the day at dinner, sitting at the table that was in my house growing up. The table from home.

Isaiah 64:7

Yet, LORD, you are
our father; we are
the clay and you
our potter:
we are all the work
of your hand.

THE MASTER POTTER

by **Melanie Rigney**

I t was the week of my forty-ninth birthday. I was where you'd never expect a woman who'd been away from her faith for thirty-three years to be, a woman who had left her husband of twenty years just one year earlier and taken a job in a city where she knew almost no one, a woman who had just filed for bankruptcy and who was having an affair.

I was teaching at a Christian writers' conference.

A friend had recommended me to the conference director, telling both the director and me that I needed to be there. It was the third Christian conference at which I'd taught. I generally went along with the flow when it came to prayers and services and dodged questions about my own faith "journey" or about my church. I would just say that I was raised Catholic. It had worked before and I had no doubt it would work with these folks, including my roommate and fellow instructor, Virelle Kidder.

Along with several other facilitators, I waited at the airport baggage claim area that Monday for Virelle, whose flight was the last of the group's to arrive. "There she is!" the conference director said, pointing to a beaming, sandy-haired elf of a woman hurrying down the hallway.

Virelle hugged the others who were waiting with

me, then said, "Hi! You must be Melanie! Hi, roomie!"

Once we arrived on campus, we went to the instructor orientation session. As we all introduced ourselves, another instructor said the next day was his birthday. And since he had, when it was my turn, I announced the fact that it would be my birthday too.

"Oh, what fun!" Virelle said, clapping her hands. "You're twins!"

The conference theme came from Isaiah 64:7: "We are the clay and you the potter." That evening, a potter and her husband, who lived in the area, were the presenters. As the potter worked at her wheel, turning a lump of clay into what would become a beautiful bowl, her husband read the Scripture aloud and offered a devotion. He asked us to think about the ways the Lord was reforming each of us. I just closed my eyes and shook my head. I was in a personal blast furnace. I felt that I had no one to turn to other than myself for survival. It wasn't that I didn't believe in God, I just didn't think the Almighty had shown any evidence that he believed in me — not for a very long time, anyway. God, reform me? It was a little late for that.

* * *

At precisely seven the next morning, my cell phone

rang. Virelle thought it was the alarm feature. But, by looking at the display, I knew it was The Man Not My Husband (TMNMH).

In my right ear was his Virginia drawl, wishing me a happy birthday and asking me if there were any good-looking ministers at the conference. In my left ear was Virelle, chirping "Happy birthday to you," from her bed, unaware that I was on the phone, let alone with TMNMH. I felt caught.

Finally, Virelle finished and headed for the bathroom. "Thank you!" I cooed. "Talk as soon as you get out, okay?"

"Okay!" she said in a happy, sing-songy voice.

"As soon as I get out of where?" TMNMH asked.

"My roommate."

"You have a roommate? Is she a minister?"

"Oh, hush!" I said louder than I meant to. "I mean, thank you for the happy birthday. That was really nice. But I have to go."

"Where do you have to go?" Virelle asked, coming out of the bathroom.

"I'm sorry! I was on the phone with someone who was wishing me happy birthday," I said. It wasn't written anywhere in the roommate code of ethics that I had to tell her who was on the other end of the telephone line.

"See? We're lining up to say happy birthday to yooooou!" she sang.

How did a woman as nice as Virelle get stuck with such a louse of a roommate, I wondered.

* * *

Later that day, my cell phone quit working. I could only deduce that service had been stopped for nonpayment of the bill. I shared the account with my husband and had sent my half of the payment, but still...

"Don't worry," Virelle said. "If you need to borrow mine, it'll be fine."

But I had a weekly conference call for my freelance editing business that evening. It generally ran nearly an hour. I certainly wasn't going to borrow her phone for that long.

Consequently, I walked to the pay phone at a gas station about a third of a mile away and made the call with a phone card amid the smells of gasoline and oil and the sound of semis pulling in and out. At the end, the others on the conference call sang happy birthday to me.

"Some happy birthday!" I thought, heading back to campus. It was nearly 10 PM. Maybe Virelle would be asleep. I carefully pushed the buttons to unlock the door. She was still up, reading her students' assignments.

She turned with a welcoming smile. "Hi, Melanie! Did your phone start working again? I was a little worried about you." There was something in her honest, trusting eyes that I couldn't ignore.

"Oh Virelle," I said, sobbing. "I need you to pray over me. My life is a disaster. I'm probably getting divorced. I don't have any money. I think my cell phone doesn't work because my husband didn't pay the bill. And I don't know what I'm doing at a Christian writers' conference. I don't even have a church."

She looked up at me without a trace of judgment and extended her hand. I clutched it and sat down by her side.

"Dear Jesus, please help your servant Melanie. She wants to come to you—I can hear it in her voice and feel it in her presence. Help her find her way. Help her find her way to her husband and let them both walk with you. Heavenly Father, thank you for all the good you do through Melanie. Let us both serve you this week and beyond. Amen."

We sat there for what seemed like a half hour, me crying and rambling, Virelle listening and nodding. Finally, I was spent. And yet, there was a calm, a peace inside me that hadn't been there for months, maybe even years. I squeezed her hand once more.

"Thank you, Virelle," I said, and started for the bathroom. Then I turned around. "How did you do that?"

"Do what?"

"Just talk to God like that for me. Maybe I'm not worth it."

"Oh, Melanie," she said, shaking her head. "Jesus came and died for our sins, and none of us deserved that. But he did it. We all fail, and will continue to fail unless and until we trust in him and invite him into our life."

*   *   *

I expected to feel uncomfortable around Virelle after that, but I didn't. Together, we cooked up a special "roast" of the conference director. Together, we attended evening devotions. Together, we attended a fundraising auction where I purchased a framed photo of the potter we had seen earlier in the week, her hands in the clay.

Our departing flights at the end of the week were far enough apart that Virelle and I would be on different shuttle runs. We hugged as she prepared to leave.

"I don't want to lose you, Virelle," I said, near tears again. "Please, can we stay in touch?"

"Absolutely! You're not getting rid of me that easily," she said with a laugh. "But I do need to say a few things before I leave. First, there's another woman I know who has a story similar to yours. Her information is on this piece of paper. You might want to talk. Second, I signed your book as you asked. I hope you enjoy it. Finally..." she hesitated ever so slightly..."I hope you'll look for Jesus when you return home." She gave me a quick hug, and then was gone.

I looked at my copy of her book *Donkeys Still Talk: Hearing God's Voice When You're Not Listening.*

"For Melanie, my new friend, sister in Christ, writing buddy, and the most soft and gentle person at [a federal agency]," she had written. "May we both bloom in the years ahead. Praying for you, Virelle."

I started to cry again, then burst into full-blown tears when I saw that Virelle had dog-eared a page for me. It was Chapter 6, titled "Unburdening the Beast."

* * *

On a weekday night two months later, I walked into a parish near my apartment. In the bulletin was an item that said a program would be starting up soon for those considering a return to Catholicism. I thought once again about what Virelle had said about inviting the

Lord into my life, and then I signed up. Four months later, I received the Eucharist for the first time in thirty-three years. It was the first Mass I'd ever attended on Christmas Day.

Within the next year, my divorce was final and I'd started writing Catholic devotions. Three years later, I'd completed bankruptcy repayments of more than $100,000. The Man Not My Husband and I parted ways.

I still have that photo of the potter's hands. It reminds me on the days that I am tempted to wallow in self-loathing that the Lord loves me and is continually remaking me, drawing me closer to him. And every time I am complimented on my ability to pray spontaneously at meals and for my friends, I give thanks to Virelle.

John 15:11

"I have told you this
so that my joy may be
in you and your joy
may be complete."

OUR GOD IS JOY

by **Stephen J. Rossetti**

As I was growing up in a small town, one day a friend of mine happened to mention the training classes he was attending for becoming an altar server. A little light went on inside me and I thought, "I want that too." So, I walked unannounced into the class and sat down amid the other young boys. The old pastor never said a thing; he just accepted me. And so, I became an altar boy.

I kept serving for several years and had become one of the senior servers when, one day, the new pastor asked me if I had thought of becoming a priest. My first thought was, "Yuucch! These priests wear black, drive black cars, and seem pretty joyless." But, here I am more than fifty years later, wearing black and serving as a priest (although I drive a white car!).

Somehow, we in Catholicism got the idea that religion is meant to be a rather dour affair. For many, it seems somber and depressing. Who would want to be a Christian, much less a priest or religious, with such a notion?

A survey of eighth-grade students conducted years ago, asked the youths to rank, in order, thirty-five jobs or vocations such as teacher, doctor, and carpenter in terms of desirability, with "saint" being one of the choices. These eighth-graders ranked "saint" as second to last. Garbage collector beat saint out for last place. When asked why they did not want to become saints, the children said that being a saint is an unhappy life. It reminds me of a saying often attributed to St. Teresa of Ávila, "From sour-faced saints, good Lord, deliver us!" Such impressions have not changed much in half a century.

SEARCHING FOR JOY

Still harboring this negative impression, when it came time for me to go to college, I went to the Air Force Academy, rather than Notre Dame, where I had also applied. While I was serving overseas in Taiwan as an intelligence officer, I met a number of missionary sisters and priests. I spent quite a bit of time with them, particularly the Maryknoll Sisters. What struck me most was their joyful spirit. They were enthusiastic about life. Materially speaking, they had very little, living as poor missionaries. They were far from home in the midst of a foreign culture. Nevertheless, they loved the Chinese people, and these women were loved by those whom they served as well.

At the same time, I still was compelled to stay close to God. I was going to daily Mass, meditating daily, and reading holy books. Slowly, some of the joy of the sisters began to seep into me. I do not remember any particular moment, but rather, it was a slow process of being filled with this joy. The real growth was gradual. But there was no question about it: joy was coming into my life.

As my time in the military neared its end, I was searching for a new way of life. Having steeped myself in the writings of the contemplatives and mystics, I tried the Carthusian hermits in Vermont, a solitary and austere order. I was impressed with their joyful spirit and their living in solitude with God.

Their founder, St. Bruno, characterized this austere life as "a peace that the world does not know and joy in the Holy Spirit." Indeed, I found that the monks were, despite their poverty and stark discipline, joyful people. There was a radiant joy about them, something that was especially evident among the older monks. In fact, the visible joy of these older monks was a manifest sign of their holiness. I, too, found much joy there living in an intense closeness with the Lord.

Their life proved a bit too much for me, however, especially because of the enclosure. And so, I left grudgingly and eventually became a diocesan priest. This realization of the gift of joy has remained with me to this day.

THE GIFT OF JOY

When I was leaving the monastery after several months, I remember getting on a bus to go back home. What struck me was how sad all the passengers were. I first thought that some tragedy had befallen them. But then I realized that nothing horrible had happened. Rather, I became aware that most people in the world were nearly always this sad, something I did not know until I had experienced a truly joyful community. I was blessed to gain a taste of the joy God meant for us all to have.

Sadly, the fullness of joy that God wants for us has been broken. The world in our time seems to be spiraling into distrust, isolation, conflict, and violence. I don't think it is an accident that, at the same time, atheism and secularism, are rising, a by-product of a world that has lost touch with its Creator.

Paul VI noted such a trend some time ago in his marvelous apostolic exhortation *Gaudete in Domino* (On Christian Joy). "This difficulty in attaining joy seem to us particularly acute today" (no. I), he wrote. "Money, comfort, hygiene and material security are often not lacking," he continued, "and yet boredom, depression and sadness unhappily remain the lot of many" (no. I). His words were prophetic.

As the world enjoys greater technological advances

and scientific developments, one would expect people to be happier. But studies show that suicide rates in the world have increased by sixty percent in the last forty-five years.

Whence comes true joy? Pope Paul VI said clearly, "It is spiritual" (no. I). Likewise, St. Paul's Letter to the Galatians speaks of joy as a fruit of the Spirit (Gal 5:22). I particularly love the gospel passage from John 15, which is the focus of this reflection, "my joy may be in you and your joy may be complete." We usually picture Jesus with a solemn visage, and often suffering on the cross. Of course, this is a central Christian image. But the passage from John suggests that Jesus was, on the whole, joyful. Jesus himself spoke of "my joy."

Paul VI noted this Scripture passage and asked the question, what was the source of Jesus' joy? His answer is illuminative: "If Jesus radiates such peace, such assurance, such happiness, such availability, it is by reason of the inexpressible love by which He knows that He is loved by His Father" (no. III).

Simply put, joy is a gift of God. Or rather, joy is part of God's very being. When God dwells in us in a deep, loving relationship, we are filled with joy because we are filled with God. Our God has revealed himself to us as joy.

JOY REDISCOVERED

I am greatly encouraged to note that God's joy and the desperate need for it today are being rediscovered in the church.

Perhaps one of the best witnesses today to true joy is the smiling face of Pope Francis himself. His joyful countenance is attractive to the world and suggests that he has personally received the gift of God's joy. In the first year of his pontificate, Pope Francis penned his apostolic exhortation *Evangelii Gaudium* (The Joy of the Gospel).

He wrote, "The great danger in today's world, pervaded as it is by consumerism, is the desolation and anguish born of a complacent yet covetous heart, the feverish pursuit of frivolous pleasures, and a blunted conscience" (no. 2). Rather, as he later wrote to the bishops, "God is present in the midst of our people. This certainty...is the source of our joy and hope." The lack of joy and the sadness and conflict that envelops our globe is rightly a central concern of our popes in modern times.

Similarly, it is becoming increasingly documented that priesthood, far from being a dour vocation, is actually one of the most fulfilling and happy lives possible. In 2009, I was given a grant to study the happiness of Catholic priests in the USA. It seemed to many people that priests were increasingly miserable, especially in the wake of the sexual abuse scandals. So we decided to investigate.

What we found was that, despite the scandals, dwindling vocations, and increasing secularism, priests were among the happiest people in the country. A surprising 92.4 percent of a sample of 2,482 priests agreed or strongly agreed that they were happy as priests.

As I began to unearth other similar studies, the results were much the same: priests are among the happiest of people. A 2006 survey of 27,000 Americans by the National Opinion Research Center found that clergy of all faiths had the highest level of job satisfaction and overall level of happiness of any jobholders.

In the United Kingdom, a 2014 government survey of people occupying 274 different jobs, found that clergy reported the very highest level of personal satisfaction. Likewise, the Center for Applied Research in the Apostolate (CARA) summarized its research in its 2012 book *Same Call, Different Men* stating that: "Given such challenges and a rather bleak outlook for future ordinations, can we presume that satisfaction among U.S. priests languishes at an all-time low? Not at all. Priests express quite high levels of satisfaction with their lives and ministry."

FINDING JOY IN OUR LIVES

All of us are "coded" to have this joy in our lives. If we do not find it, we will inevitably become frustrated and angry. But, as God's creatures, we were made for joy. So, what ought we to do to find this joy? The first step is recognizing its true source in God. Many spend a lifetime trying to find joy in the wrong places.

After recognizing that God is the true source of our joy, we can then petition God to grant us this gift, praying also that we would become truly open to receiving it. This is a prayer God will certainly answer. Let us open our hearts and make a manger ready for his coming.

There are many signs of God's presence in the world and in people around us. God's joy is "hidden," yet palpably present in our daily lives. We need only to learn to see it. I have learned through my experiences that, as our eyes are "opened" to God's presence, we taste a little bit of God's heavenly joy even now.

Pope Francis preached in a homily that joy is a true sign of a Christian. He further said, "No Christian can exist without joy," adding, "the Christian identity card is joy."

Our God is joy. I pray that God may give us this radiant joy—now and forever.

About the Authors

CHRIS KOELLHOFFER, a Sister, Servant of the Immaculate Heart of Mary, is an author and spiritual guide who offers retreats and presentations nationally and internationally. Visit www.chriskoellhofferihm.org for her blog and to learn more about her mobile spirituality ministry.

FATHER MARTIN PABLE is a Capuchin friar living in Milwaukee, WI. He is a noted retreat/spiritual director. He has written a number of books including *Remaining Catholic: Six Good Reasons for Staying in an Imperfect Church* and *What Catholics Believe and Why*.

MARY MARROCCO, lay woman and author, received her doctorate from the Toronto School of Theology and now lectures there. She is a practicing psychotherapist working with St. Macrina Counselling Services, which she co-founded, a unique Catholic/Orthodox collaboration in service of those seeking healing and wholeness. Mary is founder and director of St. Mary of Egypt Refuge, a countryside place of hospitality for those in need, which also helps facilitate Project Rachel (see http://stmarysrefuge.org).

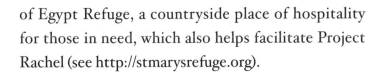

MARK NEILSEN is a former editor of *Living Faith* and is now enjoying retirement in St. Louis, MO. He continues to write for *Living Faith*. He is married and is the father of three grown children and two grandchildren.

SISTER MELANNIE SVOBODA, SND, is a Sister of Notre Dame of Chardon, OH, who gives talks and retreats nationally. Her books include *The Lord Is My Shepherd* and *Hanging onto Hope*. Visit her blog Sunflower Seeds at www.melanniesvobodasnd.org.

AMY WELBORN is a freelance writer living in Birmingham, AL, who has written many books on various elements of Catholic life: spirituality, saints, and history. Visit her website at http://www.amywelborn.com.

STEVE GIVENS is a widely published writer on Christian spirituality, a spiritual director and retreat facilitator and a composer and singer. He has been a regular contributor to *Living Faith* since 1988. You can read his blog at www.givenscreative.com.

....

PATRICIA LIVINGSTON is an award-winning speaker, author and retreat director. A wife, mother and grand-mother of nine, she lives in Tampa, FL. Her website is patricialivingston.com.

....

MELANIE RIGNEY thanks God every day for her return to Catholicism in 2005 after 33 years away. She is the author of two books about women saints, *Blessed Are You: Inspiration from Our Sisters in Faith* and *Sisterhood of Saints: Daily Guidance and Inspiration*. Visit her website at melanierigney.com.

....

MSGR. STEPHEN J. ROSSETTI, PH.D., DMIN, is a priest of the Diocese of Syracuse, NY. He is an author and licensed psychologist. He is President Emeritus of Saint Luke Institute. He teaches at The Catholic University in Washington, DC and the Gregorian University in Rome.

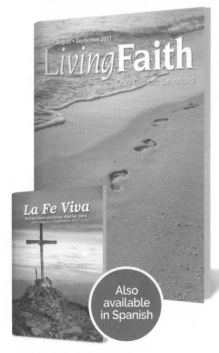
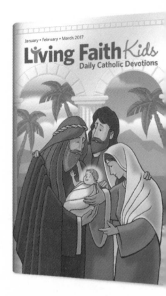